David Porteous Art and Craft Books

Flower Painting Paul Riley
Intimate Landscapes Paul Riley
Silk Painting Vibeke Born
The Dough Book Tone Bergli Joner
Fun Dough Brenda Porteous
More Fun Dough Brenda Porteous
Fairytale Doughcraft Anne Skødt
Paperworks Dette Kim
Paper Craft Dette Kim
Gift Boxes Claus Zimba Dalby
Decorative Boxes Susanne Kløjgård
Wooden Toys Ingvar Nielson
Papier Mâché Lone Halse
Pressed Flowers Pamela le Bailly
Silhouettes in Cross Stitch Julie Hasler
Cats: A Cross Stitch Alphabet Julie Hasler
Nursery Cross Stitch Julie Hasler

Nursery Cross Stitch

Nursery Cross Stitch

Julie Hasler

DAVID PORTEOUS
CHUDLEIGH · DEVON

A CIP catalogue record for this book is
available from the British Library

ISBN 1 870586 20 4

Published by
David Porteous Editions
PO Box 5
Chudleigh
Newton Abbot
Devon TQ13 0YZ

Designed by Vic Giolitto
Photography by Garth Blore
Styling by Lesley Sleeman
Printed in Singapore

CONTENTS

ACKNOWLEDGEMENTS **10**

INTRODUCTION **11**

MATERIALS AND TECHNIQUES **12**

LOOKING AFTER YOUR WORK **16**

SUPPLIERS **17**

JACK THE GIANT KILLER FRAMED PICTURE **18**

SNOW WHITE AND THE SEVEN DWARFS FRAMED PICTURE **22**

PIED PIPER AND TOM THUMB LAVENDER BAGS **26**

GEORGIE PORGIE DRESSING TABLE SET **30**

HANSEL AND GRETEL NIGHTDRESS BAG **34**

CINDERELLA STOOL **38**

THUMBELINA WASTE BIN **42**

THE TINDER BOX AND BIG, BAD WOLF CUSHIONS **45**

LITTLE RED RIDING HOOD DRAW-STRING BAG **50**

SLEEPING BEAUTY HANDKERCHIEF HOLDER **53**

HOW MRS FOX MARRIED AGAIN SERVING TRAY **57**

BAA BAA BLACK SHEEP BIB AND PLACE MAT **60**

PERSONALIZED TOWELS **64**

BORDERS AND MOTIFS **69**

STRANDED COTTON SHADE NAMES AND CONVERSION CHART **75**

ACKNOWLEDGEMENTS

I should like to thank the following people for their skilful help in sewing up the cross stitch embroideries illustrated in this book: Stella Baddeley, Lesley Buckerfield, Sue Dickenson, Angela Eardley, Joyce Formby, Christine Gorton, Odette Harrison, Maureen Hipgrave, Allison Mortley, Dawn Parmley, Lynda Potter, Louise Wells and Jenny Whitlock. Special thanks, too, to Louise Wells and Connie Woolcott for making up the pieces. Thank you all for your loyalty and hard work.

I should also like to acknowledge the help and support of the following companies, which have contributed threads, fabrics, accessories and graph paper for use in this book: DMC Creative World Ltd, H.W. Peel & Company Ltd, Framecraft Miniatures Ltd and Luxury Needlepoint. For the addresses of these and other suppliers, see page 17.

INTRODUCTION

Cross stitch is as popular now as ever it was, and more and more people have discovered that it is a satisfying and inexpensive hobby. It is the ideal decoration for not only household furnishings and linen but also children's clothes and accessories – in fact, almost anything lends itself to this type of embroidery.

Cross stitch is very easy to learn, but whether you are an experienced needleworker or whether you are just beginning to enjoy the craft you will find on the pages that follow a wealth of attractive motifs. You do not have to follow the designs exactly. You can create your own original items by choosing alternative colours, by using the motifs on different articles or even by combining motifs.

The motifs and patterns in this book were devised in an attempt to embody something of earlier times, when enduring stories such as Cinderella, the Sleeping Beauty, Thumbelina and Snow White were a magical relief from the ordinariness of the day, and the magic of the story book and nursery rhyme prevailed.

If you were privileged enough to have been brought up in a home with a separate nursery you would know that it was a separate and special place, a safe and cosy haven. Nurseries were, of course, found only in the homes of the wealthy, and it was only in the Victorian period that a special room, overseen by "nanny" came into its own. While mothers remained at a distance, it was nanny who reigned in the nursery, the practical, motherly figure who took charge of the children's daily routine.

This image of the nursery as a comfortable, stable sanctum took firm hold in the public's mind, even in the twentieth century with its changed circumstances, expectations and tastes. The echoes of the often-repeated tales of the Tinder Box, Jack the Giant Killer and the Pied Piper and long-remembered nursery rhymes such as "Baa Baa Black Sheep and "Georgie Porgie" still enchant and enthral us, reminding us that, like all good things, they still exist for us all, somewhere beyond the rainbow, far from the confines of the nursery.

MATERIALS
AND TECHNIQUES

MATERIALS

To complete the projects in this book you will need the following.

•**A small, blunt embroidery needle**. A number 24 or a number 26 will be suitable for all the projects in this book.

•**Evenweave fabric.** Use a fabric on which you can easily count the threads, both vertically and horizontally. Evenweave fabrics, such as Aida, Hardanger and Ainring, are available in a wide selection of colours – ecru, red, blue, green, yellow, for example, as well as black and white – and in a variety of thread counts. Do not use a plainweave fabric; not only is it extremely difficult to keep the stitches evenly sized, but the design will become distorted.

•**Embroidery cotton.** All the projects in this book were worked in DMC stranded cotton, the number of strands that are used depending on the fabric used. The colours and the number of threads used for the pieces illustrated are indicated for each project. A table showing the names and numbers of equivalent brands is included at the back of the book.

•**Embroidery hoop.** A circular plastic or wooden embroidery hoop, 10, 12.5 or 15cm (4, 5 or 6in) in diameter and with a screw-type tension adjuster, is ideal for cross stitch.

• **A pair of embroidery scissors.** You will need a pair of sharp, pointed scissors, which you should keep especially for sewing.

PREPARING TO WORK

To prevent the edges of the fabric from unravelling you can either protect them by folding over lengths of masking-tape along each edge or you can whip stitch each edge by hand or stay stitch the edges on a machine.

Where you make your first stitch is important because it will dictate the position of the finished design on your fabric. Find the exact centre of the chart by drawing vertical and horizontal lines from the centre points of the sides of each chart. Find the centre of your fabric by folding it in half, first vertically and then horizontally, pinching it along the folds so that the crease can be faintly seen; again, where the creases intersect is the centre of the fabric. You may wish to mark these lines with basting stitches.

You should begin your cross stitch at the top of the design. Count the squares up from the centre point and then out to the left or right as far as the first symbol. Remember that each square on the chart represents a square on your fabric, and each symbol represents a different colour. The "square" on the fabric consists of the block formed by the two lines of the cross stitch.

If you are using an embroidery hoop, place the portion of the fabric on which you are going to be working over the inner hoop and gently push the outer ring over it. Carefully and evenly pull the fabric until it is as taut as a drum in the hoop and the mesh is perfectly straight, tightening the screw as you do so. If you are right handed you will find it easier to work if the screw is in the "10 o'clock" position; if you are left handed, it should be at about "1 o'clock". This will help prevent the thread from catching in the screw as you sew. While you work you will find that you will need to tighten the screw from time to time to keep the material taut. It is easier to stitch when the fabric is under tension because you can more easily push your needle through the holes without piercing the fibres of the fabric.

When you stitch with stranded cotton, always cut off a suitable length to work with and separate the appropriate number of strands. For example, if the design calls for two strands of cotton, use two separate strands, not one strand doubled.

TECHNIQUES

Cross Stitch

To make your first stitch, bring your needle up from the wrong side of your work through a hole in the fabric (Fig. 1) at the left-hand end of a row of stitches of the same colour. Fasten the thread by holding a short length of thread on the underside of the fabric and securing it with the first two or three stitches you make (Fig. 2). Never use knots to fasten the end of your thread; they will make it impossible for the finished work to lie absolutely flat and small bumps will be visible from the front.

Fig. 1

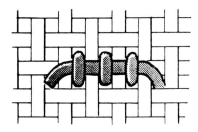

Fig. 2

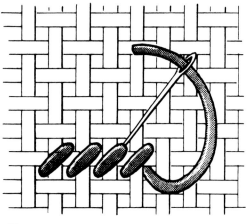

Fig. 3

Next, bring your needle across one square to the right and one square above on a left-to-right diagonal and insert it in the hole (Fig. 1). Half of the stitch is now made. Continue in this way, working across the row until you have completed the appropriate number of stitches. Your stitches should lie diagonally on the top of your work and vertically on the wrong side. Then complete the top half of your stitch by crossing back from right to left to make the "x" (Fig. 3). Work back along the row to complete all the crosses (Fig. 4). Vertical rows of stitches can be worked as shown in Fig. 5.

Cross stitch can also be worked by completing each cross as you come to it, as you would work an isolated stitch. This method works just as well. It is simply a matter of personal preference. The only point you must remember is that all the top stitches must lie in the same direction.

Finish off each length of thread by running your needle under four or more stitches on the wrong side (Fig. 6) and by cutting off the end close to your work.

Backstitch

In some of the designs backstitch is used for outlines or for some of the finer details. Work any backstitch shown on the charts when you have finished all the cross stitch.

Always use one strand fewer than you did for the cross stitch. For example, if the cross stitch was worked with three strands, you would use two strands of cotton for the backstitch. If only one strand of cotton was used for the cross stitch, you would also use one strand for the backstitch.

Backstitch is worked from hole to hole, and

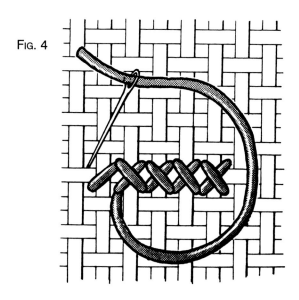

FIG. 4

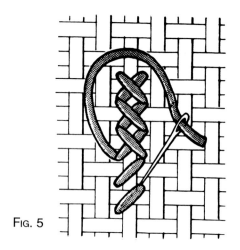

FIG. 5

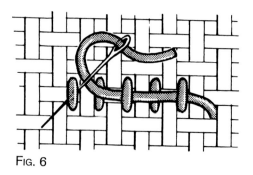

FIG. 6

14

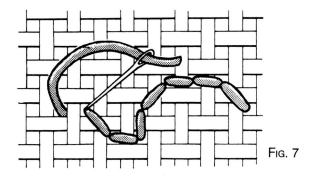

FIG. 7

you can work horizontally, vertically or diagonally (Fig. 7). Take care that you do not pull the stitches too tightly or the contrast of colour will be lost. Finish off the thread as you would for cross stitch.

TIPS

Cross stitch is one of the easiest of all stitches. For perfect results every time, bear the following points in mind as you work.

•When you are stitching take care that you do not pull the fabric out of shape. You can do this by making all your stitches in two distinct movements – straight up through a hole in the fabric and then straight down – and by keeping your fabric taut on a hoop while you work. Do not pull the thread too tight; it should lie snugly on the design, not bite into it. If you use this method you will find that the thread lies just where you want it to and will not pull the material out of shape.

•If your thread becomes twisted while you work, drop your needle and allow it to untwist itself. Do not continue to work with a twisted thread because it will look thinner and not cover the material well.

•Never leave your needle in the area of the design when it is not in use. No matter how good the needle may be, it could rust in time and mark your work permanently.

•Do not carry threads across open expanses of fabric. If you are working separate areas of the same colour, finish off and begin again. Loose threads, especially of dark colours, will be visible from the right side of the work when the project is completed.

•When you have completed the design, iron your work by placing it, right side down, on a soft towel and pressing it under a slightly damp cotton cloth.

Looking After Your Work

You may at some stage find that your projects need to be laundered. This is not a problem if you simply follow the advice given by DMC with its six-stranded cotton. The guidelines in the table below are for washing embroidered items, which should always be washed separately, and never with your other laundry.

Cotton or Linen Fabric	Synthetic Fabric
Recommended washing	
Wash in warm, soapy water. Rinse thoroughly. Squeeze without twisting and hang to dry. Iron on reverse side under two layers of white linen.	Not recommended.
Bleaching or whitening agent	
Dilute according to the manufacturer's instructions. Pre-soak the embroidery in clear water, then soak for 5 minutes in a solution of about 20ml (1 tbsp) of disinfectant in about 1 litre (2 pints) of cold water. Rinse thoroughly in cold water.	These instructions are recommended if the white of the fabric is not of a high standard. If the fabric is pure white – i.e., white with a bluish tinge – do not use a bleaching or whitening agent.
Dry cleaning	
Avoid dry cleaning. Some spot removers (benzene and trichloroethylene) can be used for small, occasional stains.	Not recommended, even for small, occasional stains.

SUPPLIERS

Brass frames, greetings cards, bell pulls, brass and wooden trays and so on are available from:

Framecraft Miniatures Ltd
372–376 Summer Lane
Hockley
Birmingham B19 3QA
UK

Ireland Needlecraft Pty Ltd
2–4 Keppel Drive
Hallam
Victoria 3803
Australia

The Embroidery Shop
Greville-Parker
286 Queen Street
Masterton
New Zealand

Anne Brinkley Designs Inc
761 Palmer Avenue
Holmdel
NJ 97733
USA

Gay Bowles Sales Inc
PO Box 1060
Janesville
WI 53547
USA

Stranded embroidery cottons and evenweave fabrics are available from:

DMC Creative World Ltd
Pullman Road
Wigston
Leicester LE8 2DY
UK

The DMC Corporation
Port Kearney Bld.
10 South Kearney
NJ 07032–0650
USA

S.A.T.C.
43 Somerset Road
P.O. Box 3868
Capetown 8000
South Africa

DMC
51–56 Carrington Road
Marrickville
New South Wales 2204
Australia

Graph paper is available from:

H.W. Peel & Company Ltd
Norwester House
Fairway Drive
Greenford
Middlesex UB6 8PW
UK

Zweigart evenweave fabrics are available from:

John Toggit Ltd
Zweigart Sales Office
Western Canal Plaza
2 Riverview Drive
Somerset NJ 08873
USA

Brasch Hobby
10 Loveday Street
P.O. 6405
Johannesburg 2000
South Africa

Footstalls, tapestry frames, fire screens, sewing frames, sewing stools and so on are available from:

Luxury Needlepoint
Rock Channel
Rye
Sussex
TN31 7HJ

JACK THE GIANT KILLER FRAMED PICTURE

The story of Jack the Giant Killer, with his magic coat, shoes, cap and sword, is a perennial favourite with children of all ages. This motif is ideal for a framed picture – the materials quoted here are sufficient for a picture measuring 35.5 x 28cm (14 x 11in) – or you could use the image to make a mat for a dressing table or adapt it for the front of a bag.

Materials

1 piece of 18-count white Aida, 43 x 35.5cm
 (17 x 14in)
DMC six-strand embroidery cotton
No. 24 or no. 26 embroidery needle
1 piece of mounting board, 35.5 x 28cm
 (14 x 11in)
Pins
Adhesive tape
Picture frame of your choice
Rust-proof tacks

1. Complete the embroidery, placing the image centrally on the fabric and using two strands of cotton for the cross stitch and one strand for the backstitch. Press your work.

2. Place the embroidery, right side down, on a clean, flat surface and place the mounting board on it, making sure that it is positioned in

the centre of the fabric and that it is perfectly straight.

3. Turn over one of the long sides and use pins to hold it in place. Secure the opposite side in the same way, pulling the material so that it straight and taut. Hold down the two sides with tape and remove the pins.

4. Turn over the two short edges, again using pins, then tape to hold down the fabric. Mitre

the corners so that they lie smoothly and neatly.

5. Insert the glass in the frame and place the embroidery behind the glass. Add the backing board provided with the frame and hold it in place with rust-proof tacks. Cover the tacks with tape to neaten the back and to prevent dust from entering the frame. For best results, take your work to a professional framer.

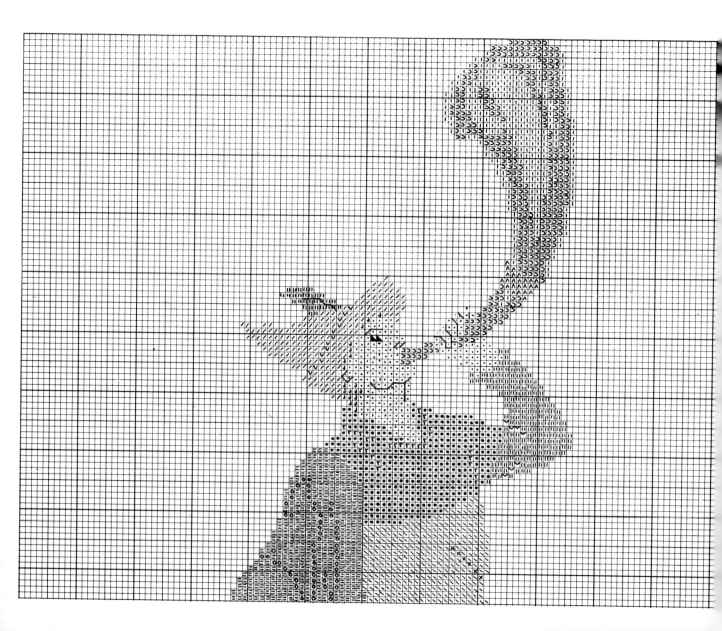

3023 (light brown grey)

3024 (very light brown grey)

326 (very deep rose red)

349 (red)

838 (very dark beige brown)

3031 (very dark brown)

611 (dark drab brown)

680 (dark old gold)

677 (very light old gold)

608 (bright orange)

898 (very dark coffee brown)

948 (very light peach)
with backstitch in
352 (mid-peach)

210 (mid-lavender)

335 (dark pink)
with backstitch in 326
(very deep rose red)

433 (mid-brown)

gold thread

327 (mid-antique lilac)

3348 (light yellow–green)

729 (mid-old gold)

3325 (baby blue)
backstitch eyebrow in
3031 (very dark brown)

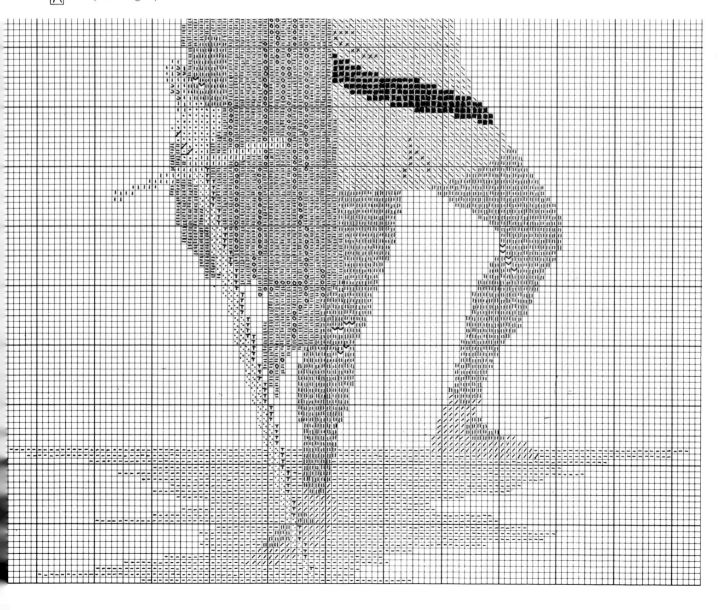

SNOW WHITE AND THE SEVEN DWARFS FRAMED PICTURE

This framed picture is made in exactly the same way as the Jack the Giant Killer picture, although it is worked on fabric with a slightly looser weave, so you should use three strands of cotton for the cross stitch and two strands for the backstitch.

Materials

1 piece of 14-count sage green Aida,
   43 x 35.5cm (17 x 14in)
DMC six-strand embroidery cotton
No. 24 or no. 26 embroidery needle
1 piece of mounting board, 35.5 x 28cm
   (14 x 11in)
Pins
Adhesive tape
Picture frame of your choice
Rust-proof tacks

See instructions on pages 18–20.

H	311 (mid-navy blue)
\	334 (mid-baby blue)
Z	937 (dark avocado green)
X	320 (mid-pistachio green)
·	948 (very light peach) with backstitch in 352 (mid-peach)
/	white
7	352 (mid-peach)
V	415 (pale grey)
●	310 (black)
∧	317 (mid-steel grey)
||	783 (Christmas gold)
8	780 (very dark topaz brown)
6	550 (very dark violet)
—	553 (mid-violet)
C	470 (mid-avocado green)
I	666 (bright Christmas red)
=	435 (very light brown)
+	814 (dark garnet red)
O	433 (mid-brown)
.·	722 (pale orange)
G	720 (dark orange)

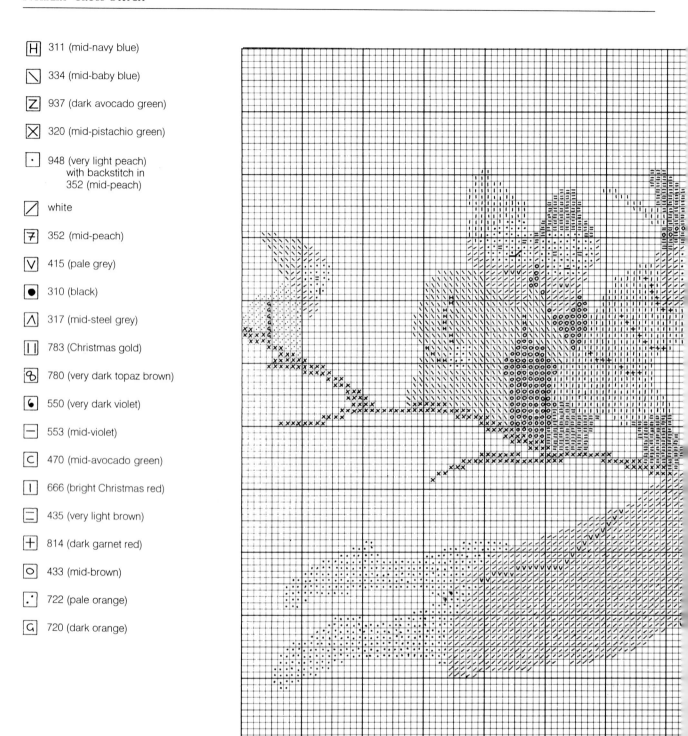

PIED PIPER AND TOMTHUMB LAVENDER BAGS

These dainty, lace-trimmed lavender bags are far too pretty to be hidden away inside a wardrobe. Hang them on your dressing-table mirror or from your bed-post so that your whole room is filled with the summery fragrance. The materials quoted here are sufficient for one bag, and the fabric measurements include a seam allowance of 12mm (1/2in).

Materials

2 pieces of 20-count, silver-flecked Bellana, each 23 x 23cm (9 x 9in)
DMC six-strand embroidery cotton
No. 26 embroidery needle
33cm (13in) white ribbon, 6mm (1/4in) wide
1.5m (5ft) white lace, 2.5cm (1in) wide
Pins
Small amount of dried lavender
Small amount of kapok or polyester stuffing
Sewing thread to match fabric
Clear, all-purpose adhesive

1. Complete the embroidery, placing the motif centrally on one piece of fabric and using one strand of cotton throughout. Lightly press your finished work.
2. Position the ribbon and lace on the Bellana, placing them just over the stitching line. Making sure that the lace does not get caught up, pin and baste the lace and ribbon in place. Remove the pins.

3. Place the other square of fabric over the first, right sides facing, and pin and tack in position.

4. Machine or hand stitch right around the sides, leaving an opening of about 4cm (1½in) in one side. Remove the pins and basting stitches.

5. Use a small piece of lining material to make a small bag for the lavender and either catch it to the bag or glue it in place.

6. Turn the bag to the right side and fill it with kapok or polyester stuffing, using small pinches at a time so that it is even. Hand stitch the opening together.

II	945 (light apricot) with backstitch in 758 (pale brick red)		/	869 (hazelnut brown)
V	890 (very dark evergreen)		.	948 (very light peach)
O	911 (mid-emerald green)		7	352 (mid-peach)
X	729 (mid-old gold)		∧	758 (pale brick red)
■	809 (Delft blue)		6	310 (black)
●	814 (dark garnet red)		Z	white
=	666 (bright Christmas red)		I	224 (light rose pink)
C	610 (very dark drab brown)		\	783 (Christmas gold)
			I	738 (very light tan)

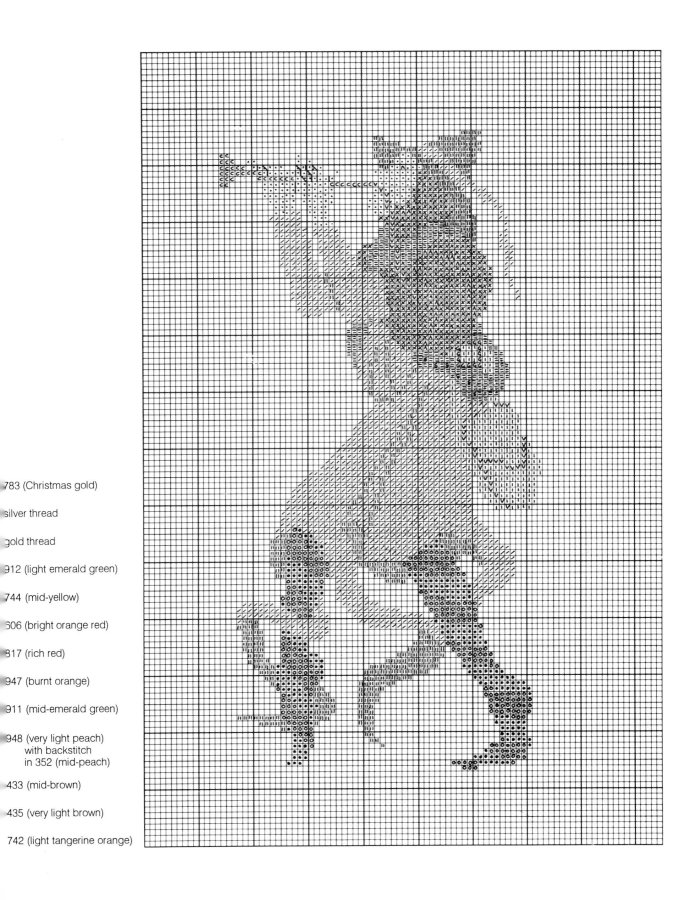

783 (Christmas gold)

silver thread

gold thread

912 (light emerald green)

744 (mid-yellow)

606 (bright orange red)

817 (rich red)

947 (burnt orange)

911 (mid-emerald green)

948 (very light peach)
    with backstitch
    in 352 (mid-peach)

433 (mid-brown)

435 (very light brown)

742 (light tangerine orange)

GEORGIE PORGIE DRESSING TABLE SET

This pretty dressing table set featuring Georgie Porgie would be a pretty addition to any bedroom. The motif would be suitable for a shoe bag, or you could work it on a piece of fabric that you then stitched to the pocket of a dressing gown.

Materials

1 piece of 25-count blue Lugana, 41 x 26.5cm (16¼ x 10½in)
2 pieces of 25-count blue Lugana, each 22 x 22cm (8½ x 8½in)
DMC six-strand embroidery cotton
No. 26 embroidery needle

1. Complete the motifs, placing them centrally on the fabric, using three strands of cotton for the cross stitch and two strands for the backstitch, which should be worked over two threads of the fabric, making it, in effect, 13 stitches to the inch. Press, from the wrong side, if you wish.

2. Make a decorative fringe by fraying the edges of the fabric for about 12mm (½in). Do this by removing the threads one at a time.

	white	

II	white
·	948 (very light peach) with backstitch in 352 (mid-peach)
O	666 (bright Christmas red)
◢	816 (garnet red)
V	471 (light avocado green)
/	435 (very light brown)
X	433 (mid-brown)
■	310 (black)
◖	823 (dark navy blue)
=	797 (royal blue)
Λ	415 (pale grey)
I	726 (light topaz yellow)
Z	742 (light tangerine orange)
\	434 (light brown)
—	676 (light old gold)
⟩	680 (dark old gold)
●	300 (very dark mahogany brown)
+	800 (pale Delft blue)
C	352 (mid-peach)

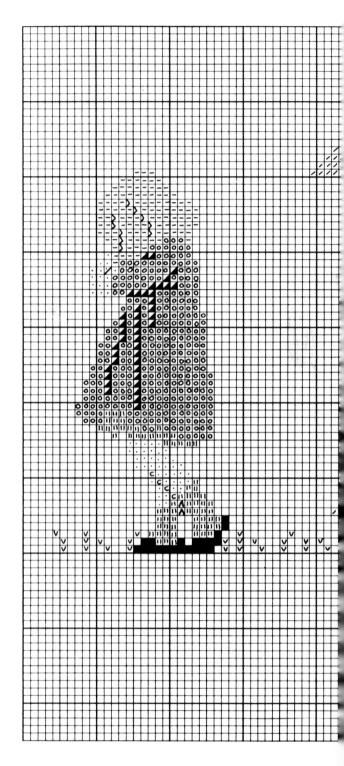

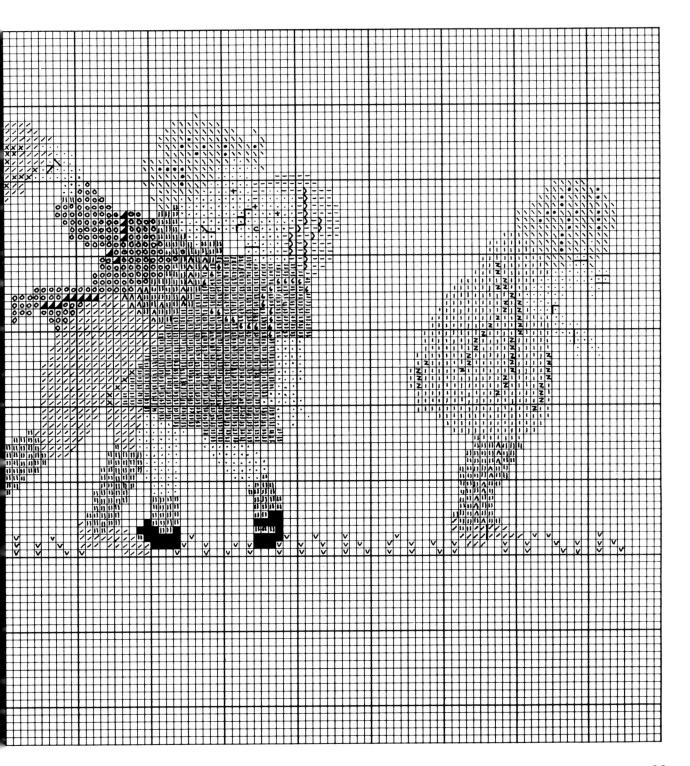

HANSEL AND GRETEL NIGHTDRESS BAG

This useful nightdress bag is large enough to hold a child's long nightdress or a pair of pyjamas. It has a draw-string top and could also be used as a shoe bag or for toys. The fabric measurements quoted below include a seam allowance of 12mm (½in).

Materials

2 pieces of 27-count beige Linda, each approximately 48.5 x 38cm (19 x 15in)

DMC six-strand embroidery cotton

No. 26 embroidery needle

2 pieces of cream lining fabric, each approximately 43 x 33cm (17 x 13in)

Sewing thread to match fabric

2m (6ft 6in) beige ribbon, 2.5cm (1in) wide

1. Complete the cross stitch embroidery, placing it so that there is room for the seam allowance at the sides and at the bottom of the motif. Use two strands for the cross stitch and one strand for the backstitch.

2. Place the two pieces of Linda together, right sides facing, then pin and baste them together. Stitch one side seam down from the top for 4cm (1½in). Leave a gap of 3cm (1¼in), then sew to the bottom. Sew across the bottom and repeat for the other side (see Fig. 8).

3. Press open the side seams around the gaps and top stitch 6mm (¼in) around the openings (see Fig. 9).

4. Turn to the right side and press, taking care not to iron over the embroidery.

5. Make the lining by placing the two pieces of lining fabric together, right sides facing. Stitch the side seams, then stitch the bottom seam, leaving an opening of about 10cm (4in) through which to turn the lining the other way out (see Fig. 10). Do not turn yet.

6. Place the outer bag inside the lining so that the right sides are facing. Stitch around the top edge.

7. Turn the bag the right way out through the gap in the bottom of the lining. Hand stitch the gap in the lining.

8. Press the top edge of the bag along the seam, then top stitch around the bag 6mm (¼in) above the ribbon opening and again below the opening (see Fig. 11).

9. Cut the ribbon into two equal lengths and thread both pieces through the casement formed by the two parallel rows of stitches. Stitch the ends of each length of the ribbon together.

Symbol	Code	Description
:·	640	(very dark beige grey)
Z	809	(Delft blue)
≡	644	(mid-beige grey)
/	3325	(baby blue)
O	747	(very light sky blue)
X	318	(light steel grey)
■	310	(black)
II		white
●	722	(pale orange) with backstitch in 720 (dark orange)
◢	720	(dark orange)
·	948	(very light peach) with backstitch in 352 (mid-peach)
—	3688	(mid-mauve)
∧	3685	(dark mauve)
V	781	(dark topaz brown)
I	932	(light antique blue)
6	930	(dark antique blue)
C	433	(mid-brown) with backstitch in 938 (dark forest brown)
G	368	(light pistachio green)
\	319	(dark green)

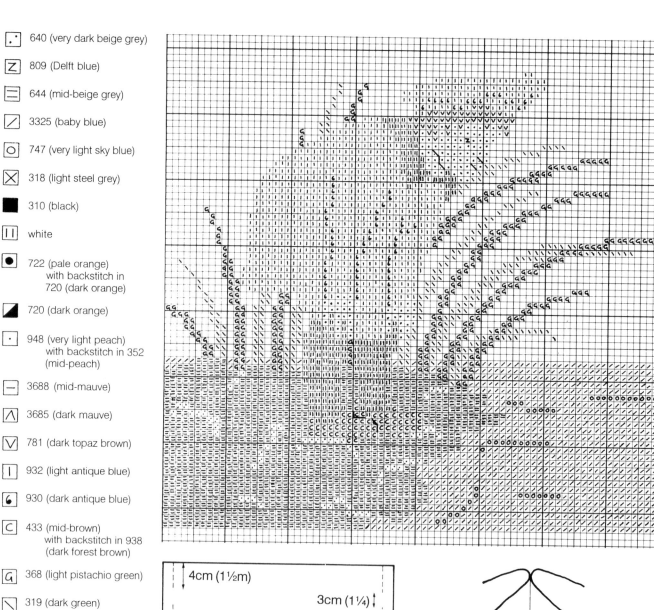

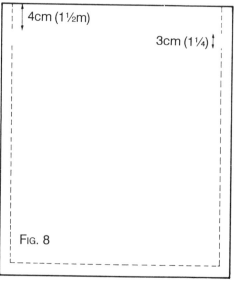

4cm (1½m)

3cm (1¼)

Fig. 8

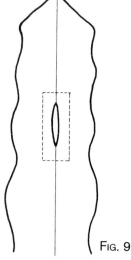

Fig. 9

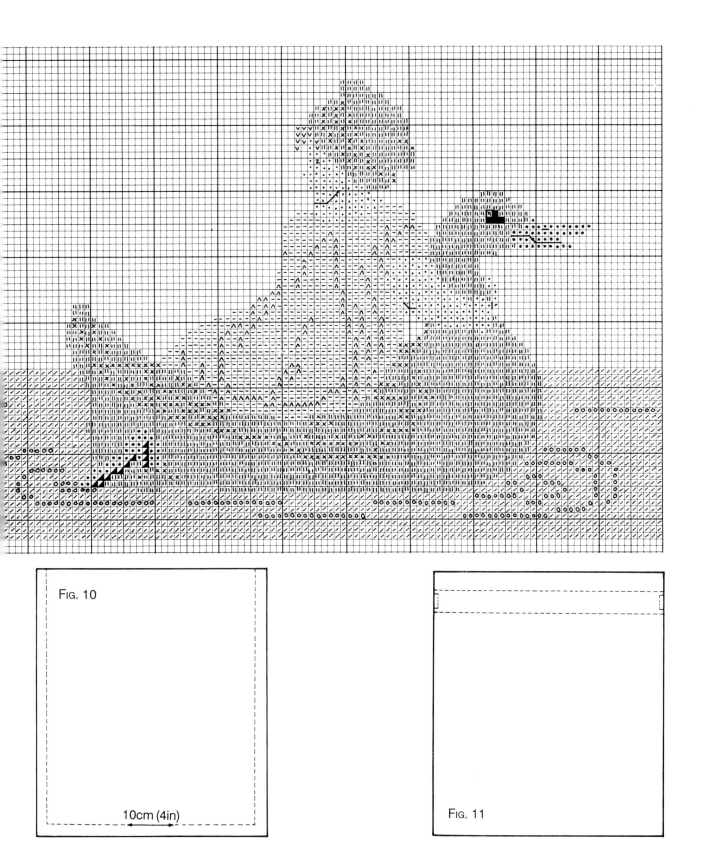

Fig. 10

10cm (4in)

Fig. 11

CINDERELLA STOOL

This stool is one of the range of attractive self-upholster furniture that is now available from many good craft suppliers and department stores. All these pieces are sold ready for you to fit with a piece of embroidery or fabric of your choice. The stool illustrated here will take a needle-work design measuring 35.5 x 35.5cm (14 x 14in).

Materials

1 piece of 14-count sage green Aida, 52 x 52cm (20½ x 20½in)
DMC six-strand embroidery cotton
No. 24 embroidery needle
1 small self-cover stool
1 piece of calico, 52 x 52cm (20½ x 20½in)
6mm (¼in) rust-proof tacks, a staple gun or thin twine

1. Complete the cross stitch embroidery, centring the design on the fabric and using three strands of cotton for the cross stitch and two strands for the backstitch.
2. These stools are made to accept needlepoint designs, which are worked on canvas which is thicker than the evenweave fabric we have used. You should, therefore, cover the top of the stool with calico or a similar firm cotton before you begin so that the embroidery fits snugly. To cover the stool with calico, follow the directions given below for the embroidery.

3. Remove the top of the stool by undoing the screws that are recessed under the frame. Put the screws in a safe place while you work.

4. Lay the top of the stool on a flat surface with the pad facing upwards. Use a fabric tape measure to measure the width (from side to side) and the depth (from back to front) of the top, making sure that you allow for the curve. Add 7.5cm (3in) to each dimension.

5. Lay the finished embroidery, right side down, on a flat, clean surface and make sure it will fit over the top of the stool with the embroidered design in the centre.

6. Turn down a hem of 6mm (¼in) on all four edges. Pin and baste into place. Remove the pins.

7. Lay the embroidery, right side down, on a flat, clean surface and place the pad, face down, on the work so that an equal amount of material is visible on all sides.

8. Press the pad down on to the material along one edge. You may have to kneel on it if you are working alone or ask a friend to help you. Bring the material over the edge and secure it in position with 6mm (¼in) tacks. Make sure

that the tacks go through the hemmed edge. Keep the material straight as you work, placing the tacks in the centre, then at each end, then evenly in the spaces between until there are tacks along the edge about 3cm (1¼in) apart.

9. Repeat the process along the opposite edge, pulling the material tightly and evenly into place.

10. Squeeze the pad down over one of the remaining edges, fastening the material in place as before. Mitre the fabric at the corners, so that it forms neat little creases and so that the fabric does not bulge outwards.

11. Repeat the process at the other side.

12. Alternatively, use a staple gun to hold the material in place or use thin twine or strong upholstery thread to lace the opposite sides in place.

13. If you wish, glue or sew a piece of calico or similar material under the pad to cover the tacked edges and to give a neat appearance.

14. Replace the top of the stool, gently pressing it in the corners, where the fit will be tight. Re-screw the top to the frame.

∕ 729 (mid-old gold)	I 322 (dark baby blue)	O 407 (mid-cocoa brown) with backstitch in 310 (black)
6 676 (light old gold)	X 311 (mid-navy blue)	═ 642 (dark beige grey)
· 948 (very light peach) with backstitch in 352 (mid-peach)	— white	V 310 (black)
◢ 809 (Delft blue)	∧ 415 (pale grey)	‖ 722 (pale orange)
⌀ 352 (mid-peach)	C 644 (mid-beige grey) with backstitch in 340 (periwinkle blue)	● 720 (dark orange)
7 353 (peach)		■ 3347 (mid-yellow–green)

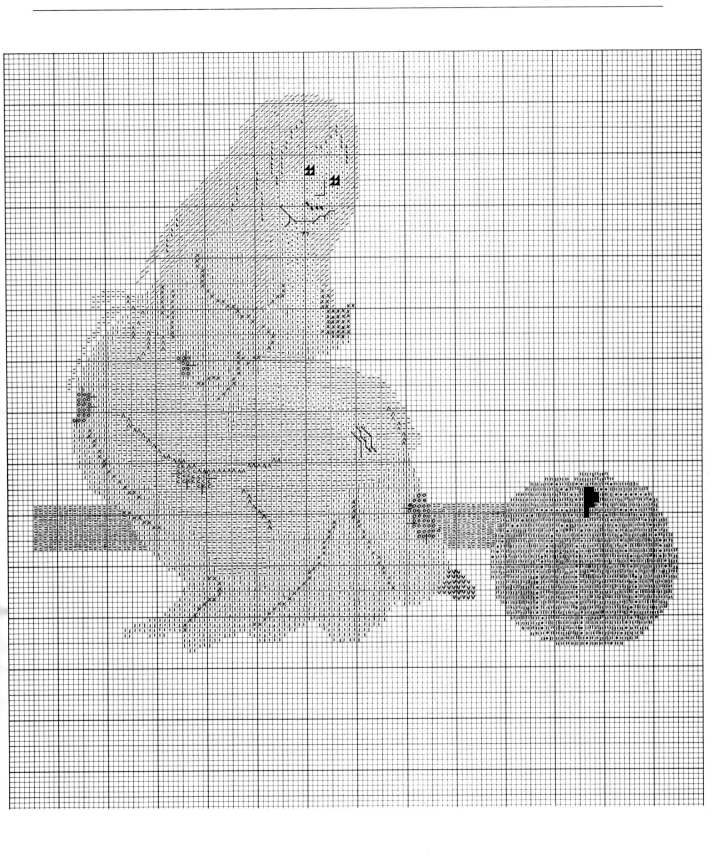

THUMBELINA WASTE BIN

We have used this pretty little design on a piece of fabric that wraps around a waste-paper basket, making it ideal for a girl's bedroom. You can buy plain, straight-sided waste-paper bins, but if your bin has sloping sides, you will have to trim away the material at the back so that the seam lies neatly and adjust the position of the motif so that it lies parallel with the base of the bin.

Materials
1 plain, straight-sided waste bin
1 piece 18-count white Aida, wide enough to
 wrap around circumference plus 2.5cm
 (1in) and as deep as the bin, plus a 12mm
 (½in) hem at top and bottom
DMC six-strand embroidery cotton
No. 26 embroidery needle
White sewing cotton
Clear, all-purpose adhesive

1. Complete the embroidery, placing the design centrally on the Aida and using two strands of cotton for the cross stitch and one strand for the backstitch.
2. Turn in, pin and baste a 12mm (½in) hem on all four edges. Check the fit around the bin, then machine stitch around the edges to give a firm, neat finish.
3. Carefully glue the finished piece to the bin using a clear adhesive. If you wish, oversew the back seam by hand for extra durability.

⊟ 352 (mid-peach)	◉ 318 (light steel grey)	∧ 353 (peach)	◤ 351 (dark peach)
◉ 435 (very light brown)	◥ 793 (blue)	· 948 (very light peach)	■ 310 (black)
✕ 350 (light red)	∨ 726 (light topaz yellow)	∣ 437 (light tan brown)	C 523 (mid-olive green) backstitch around eyes in 352 (mid-peach)
╱ 930 (dark antique blue)	∥ 791 (deep royal blue)	⋰ white	

THE TINDER BOX AND BIG, BAD WOLF CUSHIONS

*These pretty lace-edged cushions are ideal for a bed or a
favourite chair in a child's room. They are easy to make,
and you could easily use one of the other motifs in this book.
The materials quoted here are sufficient to make one cushion, 28cm (11in) across and with a seam allowance
of 12mm (½in).*

Materials

1 piece of 18-count blue Aida, 30.5 x 30.5cm
  (12 x 12in)
DMC six-strand embroidery cotton
No. 26 embroidery needle
Compasses and a soft pencil
1 piece of contrasting fabric, 30.5 x 30.5cm
  (12 x 12in), to back the cushion
Sewing thread to match the fabric
91cm (36in) pre-gathered white lace, 4cm
  (1½in) deep
1 cushion pad, 28cm (11in) in diameter

1. Complete the embroidery, placing it centrally on the Aida and using two strands for the
cross stitch and one strand for the backstitch.
Press your work if necessary.

2. Place the finished piece face down on a
clean, flat surface and use compasses and a
soft pencil to draw a circle with a diameter of
28cm (11in). Cut out the circle.

3. Pin, then baste, the lace to the Aida, making
sure the edge is just over the stitching line.

4. Cut out the backing fabric in the same way
and place it on the Aida, right sides facing. Pin
and baste the two pieces together, taking care
that you do not catch the lace in the seam.

5. Machine stitch the two pieces together,
leaving an opening of about 20cm (8in).
Remove all pins and tacking stitches and turn
the cushion cover to the right side.

6. Press in the seam allowance on the open
edge, place the cushion pad inside the cover
and oversew the open edge by hand.

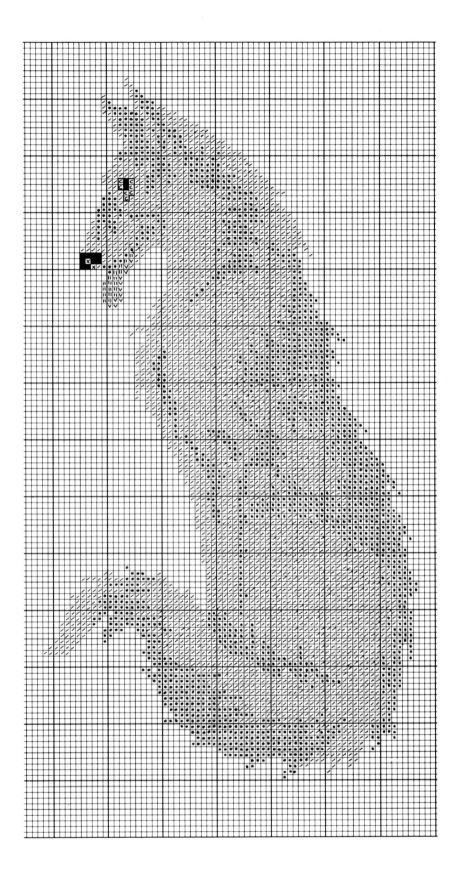

/ 642 (dark beige grey)

● 3371 (very dark forest brown)

C 743 (dark yellow)
  with backstitch in 310 (black)

■ 310 (black)

✕ 414 (steel grey)

|| 754 (light peach)

V 352 (mid-peach)

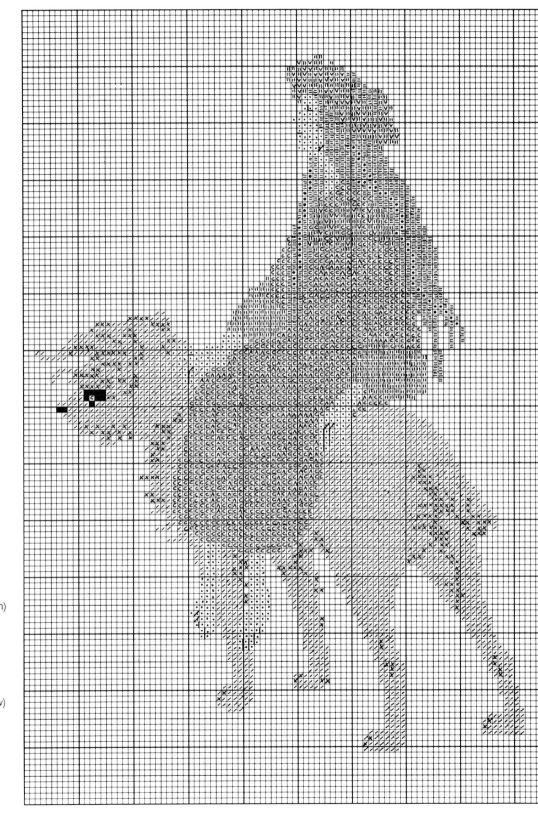

Symbol	Color
V	725 (topaz yellow)
●	680 (dark old gold)
■	310 (black)
╱	729 (mid-old gold)
✕	780 (very dark topaz brown)
·	948 (very light peach) with backstitch in 352 (mid-peach)
‖	727 (very light topaz yellow)
═	676 (light old gold)
C	white
∧	415 (pale grey)

LITTLE RED RIDING HOOD DRAW-STRING BAG

This little draw-string bag is perfect for holding cotton wool balls, and it will make a pretty and useful gift for anyone who has a new baby. The measurements given below include seam allowances of 12mm (½in).

Materials

1 piece of 18-count white Aida, 26.5 x
   40.5cm (10½ x 16in)
1 circle of 18-count white Aida, 14cm
   (5½in) in diameter
DMC six-strand embroidery cotton
No. 26 embroidery needle
White sewing thread
76cm (30in) ribbon, 6mm (¼in) wide

1. Oversew the raw edges of both pieces of Aida, either by hand or by machine, to prevent them from fraying. Press them if required.
2. Complete the embroidery, using two strands of cotton for the cross stitch and one strand for the backstitch, positioning the motif in the centre of the rectangle of Aida, 4cm (1½in) up from the bottom edge.
3. Fold the embroidered rectangle in half, with right sides together, and pin and baste the short side seam. Machine stitch down from the top edge for 2.5cm (1in), leave a gap of 12mm (½in) and continue to stitch to the bottom edge.

4. Pin and baste the circle to the bottom of the bag. Machine stitch in place, easing the seam to fit, then turn the bag to the right side.

5. At the top edge of the bag, press under 6mm (¼in) of fabric. Turn over 2cm (¾in) to form a casement for the ribbon. Machine or hand stitch along the bottom edge of the turned-down edge.

6. Thread the ribbon through the casement and stitch or tie the ends together.

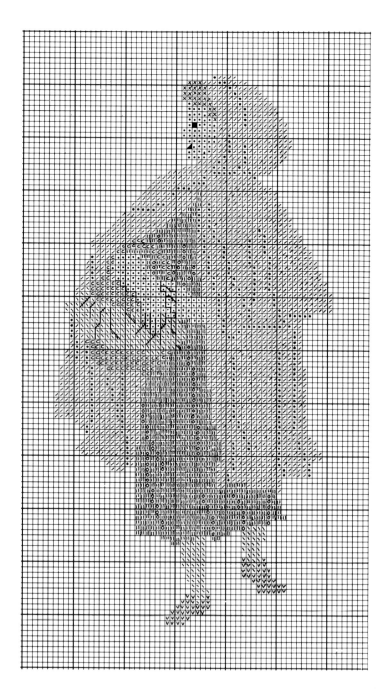

Symbol	Thread
╱	606 (bright orange red)
●	304 (mid-Christmas red)
‖	727 (very light topaz yellow)
O	725 (topaz yellow)
■	800 (pale Delft blue)
·	948 (very light peach) with backstitch in 352 (mid-peach)
⊠	676 (light old gold)
ⅴ	310 (black)
C	729 (mid-old gold)
╲	white with backstitch in 318 (light steel grey)
◢	352 (mid-peach)

SLEEPING BEAUTY HANDKERCHIEF HOLDER

This unusual handkerchief holder could also double as a desk tidy, or you could keep it on your dressing table with your hairbrushes and combs.

Materials

1 piece 18-count blue Aida, 33.5 x 28.5cm
  (13¼ x 11¼in)
DMC six-strand embroidery cotton
No. 26 embroidery needle
1 piece of iron-on Vilene, 33.5 x 28.5cm
  (13¼ x 11¼in)
1 cylindrical tin, approximately 23cm (9in)
  high and with a circumference of approximately 33cm (13in)
Double-sided adhesive tape
Sewing thread to match fabric
Clear, all-purpose adhesive

1. Complete the embroidery, placing the motif centrally on the Aida and about 4cm (1½in) up from the bottom edge. Use two strands of cotton for the cross stitch and one strand for the back stitch. Press lightly if necessary, then back with the iron-on Vilene to prevent the edges from fraying.

2. Place strips of double-sided adhesive tape around the top and bottom edges of the tin. Carefully line up the bottom edge of the tin with the edge of the Aida, making sure it is perfectly level.

3. Firmly roll the tin round over the fabric, making sure that it sticks to the tape along both edges. The fabric should meet at the back edge of the tin. Neatly but firmly lace the edges of the fabric together at the back. Turn over the surplus fabric at the top and base of the tin, using either more tape or all-purpose adhesive to keep it in place.

● 310 (black) with backstitch in 317 (mid-steel grey)	╱ 727 (very light topaz yellow) with backstitch in 783 (Christmas gold)	■ 310 (black)	O 3047 (pale golden wheat) with backstitch in 976 (golden brown)
7 352 (mid-peach)	‖ 801 (dark coffee brown)	● 975 (dark golden brown)	6 725 (topaz yellow)
· 948 (very light peach) with backstitch in 352 (mid-peach)	O 435 (very light brown) with backstitch in 801 (dark coffee brown)	✕ 334 (mid-baby blue)	V 815 (mid-garnet red)
I white	∧ 433 (mid-brown)	╱ 3325 (baby blue)	— 321 (Christmas red)
■ gold thread		‖ 976 (mid-golden brown) with backstitch in 300 (very dark mahogany brown)	= white
			▷ 415 (pale grey)

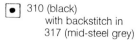

HOW MRS FOX MARRIED AGAIN
SERVING TRAY

*When your friends come to tea, impress them with this wooden tray, one of a range
specially made to take hand-stitched work. The tray measures
30.5 x 23cm (12 x 9in) and has an oval cut out for the motif. When the
embroidery is mounted under glass, it will not become soiled or stained.
See page 17 for Suppliers.*

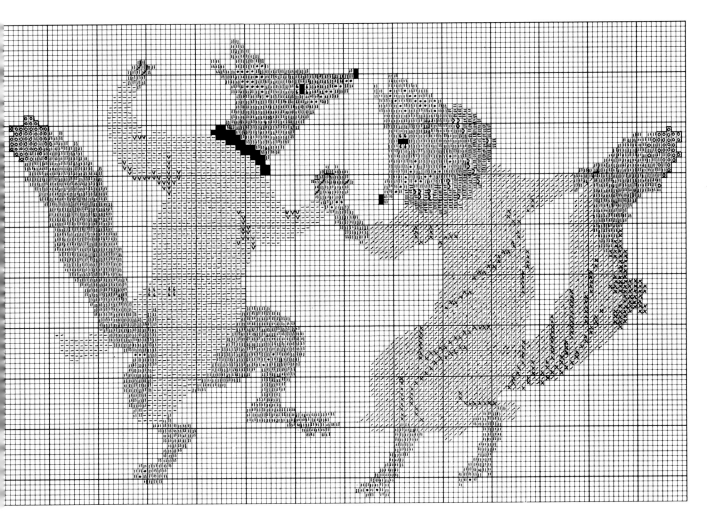

Materials
1 piece of 22-count ecru Hardanger,
  38 x 30.5cm (15 x 12in)
DMC six-strand embroidery cotton
No. 26 embroidery needle
Adhesive tape
1 wooden serving tray

1. Complete the embroidery, placing it centrally on the fabric and using one strand of embroidery cotton throughout. Press, from the wrong side, if you wish.

2. Lay the fabric, with the motif face down, on a clean, flat surface and place the piece of thick card provided with the tray in the centre. Working from one side and then the opposite side, turn the excess fabric down and hold it in place with tape.

3. When you are sure that the design is centred and the fabric is taut, secure the corners firmly and insert the mounted embroidery into the tray, following the manufacturer's instructions.

Baa Baa Black Sheep Bib and Place Mat

Keep baby interested at meal times with this bib and high-chair place mat illustrating the Baa Baa Black Sheep nursery rhyme. Although we have used red binding to trim the pieces, royal blue would be equally attractive.

Materials

1 piece of 22-count white Hardanger, 26 x 26cm (10¼ x 10¼in), for the bib 1 piece of 22-count Hardanger, 33.5 x 22.5cm (13¼ x 8½in), for the mat
DMC six-strand embroidery cotton
No. 26 embroidery needle
Greaseproof or tracing paper
Bias binding
Sewing thread to match bias binding

1. Complete the motifs, placing them on the pieces of Hardanger in the positions you wish and using one strand of cotton throughout. Press, from the wrong side, if necessary.

2. Transfer the bib pattern to tracing paper or greaseproof paper and cut around it. Pin the template to the embroidered Hardanger and cut out the shape.

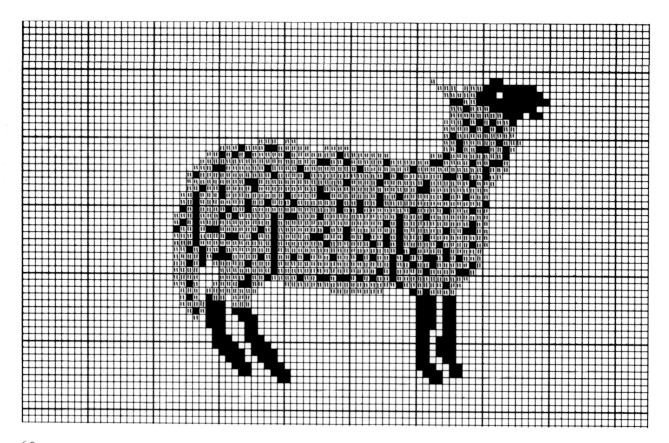

3. Round the edges of the mat by placing an upturned saucer over each corner and drawing around the curve with a soft pencil. Trim neatly to these lines.

4. Stitch bias binding all round both the bib and the mat, remembering to add two 20cm (8in) ties to the top edge of the bib.

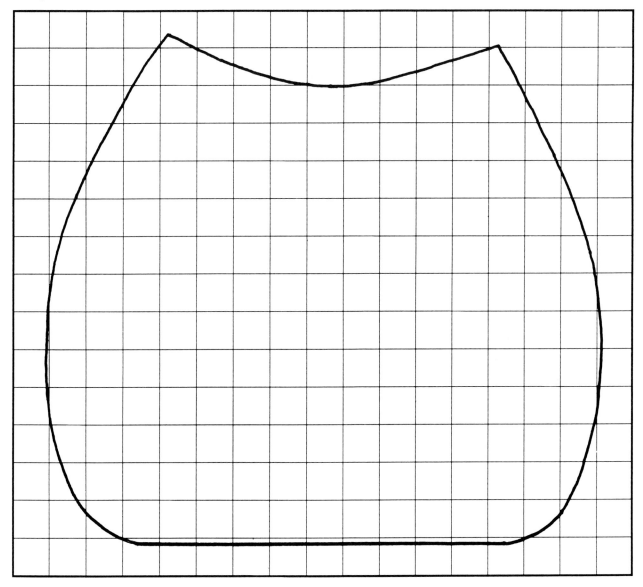

■ 310 (black)

|⊓| 317 (mid-steel grey)

PERSONALIZED TOWELS

Children of any age will be delighted to receive a personalized towel as a gift. You can embroider a name or an animal or other motif that they particularly like. You could even combine the two. The Zweigart Aida bands we have used are 5cm (2in) deep and they are available from DMC stockists (see also Suppliers on page 17). The bands are white, with edgings of blue, brown, red, cream, gold, green, pink, silver, sky blue, white or yellow. We chose the sky blue, pink and yellow edgings to match the towels.

Materials

1 piece of Zweigart Aida band, 5cm (2in)
  wide and 2.5cm (1in) longer than the width
  of your towel
DMC six-strand embroidery cotton
No. 26 embroidery needle
Towels of your choice
White sewing thread

1. Complete your chosen cross stitch design, placing it centrally on the width of the Aida band and leaving approximately 12mm (½in) unworked fabric at each end. Use two strands of cotton for the cross stitch and one strand of cotton for the backstitch.

2. Turn under a double hem at each end. Pin and baste the band to the towel in the desired position. Machine stitch the band to the towel.

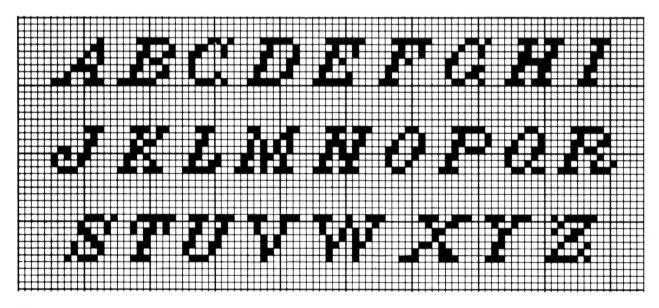

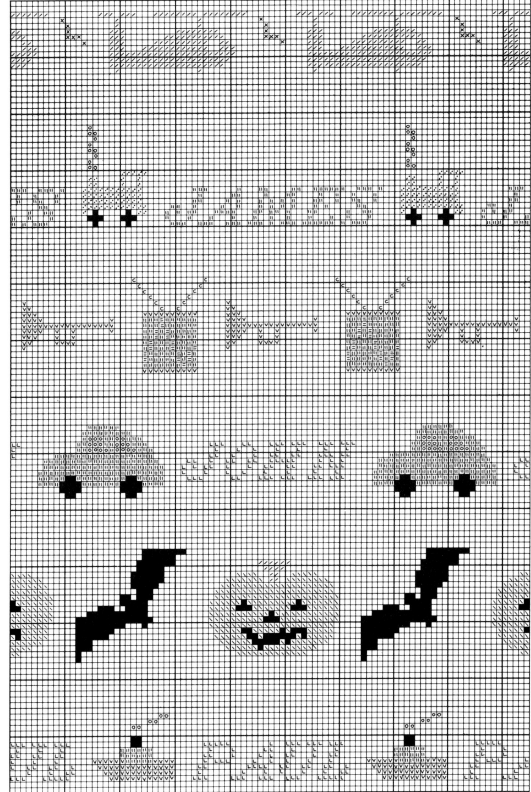

364 (light loden green)

09 (Delft blue)

666 (bright Christmas red)

10 (black)

700 (bright Christmas green)

18 (light steel grey)

783 (Christmas gold)

780 (very dark topaz brown)

676 (light old gold)

799 (mid-Delft blue)

3340 (melon orange)

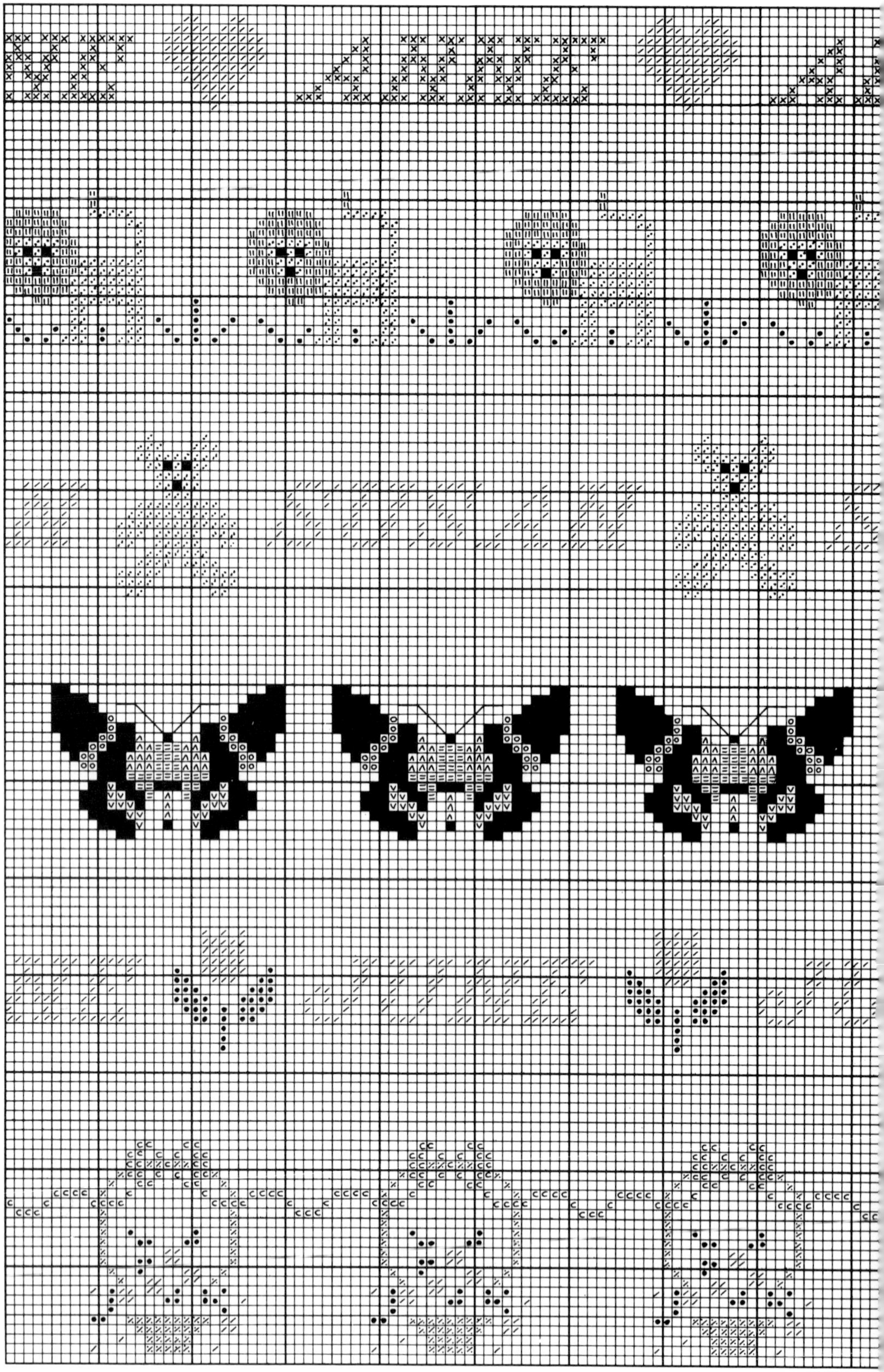

■	310 (black)
⁄	604 (light cranberry)
X	553 (mid-violet)
II	781 (dark topaz brown)
⁚	783 (Christmas gold)
●	911 (mid-emerald green)
V	349 (red)
O	3340 (melon orange)
Λ	959 (aqua)
☰	798 (dark Delft blue)
C	809 (Delft blue)
⁒	436 (tan brown)

Borders and Motifs

Using disposable waste canvas has made stitching designs onto all kinds of materials so simple that it is tempting to use it on everything. Try adding these lovely designs to children's clothes or to bed linen.

Materials

14-count waste canvas
Basting thread
DMC six-strand embroidery cotton
No. 24 embroidery needle
Pair of fine tweezers
Spray-bottle of water

1. Determine the finished size of your chosen design and cut out a piece of waste canvas that is about 4cm (1½in) wider and deeper than the finished motif.

2. Align the blue threads in the waste canvas vertically or horizontally with the weave of the fabric on which you are stitching the design. Alternatively, align the waste canvas with a seam of the garment.

3. Pin, then baste the waste canvas into position, making sure that you stitch it down all round so that it cannot move. Remove the pins.

4. Treat each pair of canvas threads as a single thread, and stitch the design as you would on any other evenweave fabric. Begin from the top of the design and work downwards, using two strands for the cross stitch and one strand for the backstitch.

5. Start and finish off the threads in the normal way – that is, by anchoring the starting thread under the first few stitches and by threading the ends back under four or five stitches. However, if you are adding a motif to a garment that will be washed often, you may want to begin and end threads with a small knot for added security.

6. When you have completed the embroidery, cut away the excess canvas, leaving about 12mm (½in) all round. Spray the embroidery from the front lightly with warm water. Do not soak it. You are aiming to dampen it sufficiently for the size in the canvas to soften.

7. Use fine tweezers to pull out the canvas strands one by one. Resist the temptation to pull more than one out at a time – if you do, you will damage your embroidery. You may have to dampen your work from time to time.

8. When all the canvas threads have been removed, your embroidered motif is left on the garment or fabric – as if by magic. Place the finished piece, right side down, on a soft, dry towel and press it lightly, taking care that you do not flatten the stitches.

9. If you stitch a design on a fabric that has to be dry cleaned, the canvas threads can be softened by rubbing them gently together. Take care, or you will damage your stitches, but it should be possible to remove each canvas thread, one at a time, without having to use water.

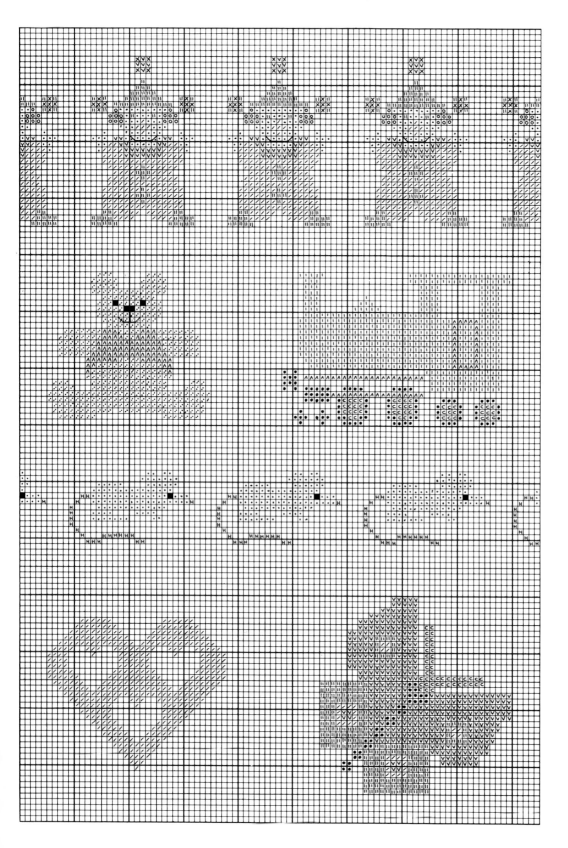

/ 603 (cranberry)
and backstitch on
clown's mouth

II 826 (mid-blue)

· white

O 970 (light pumpkin orange)

V 552 (dark violet)

X 444 (dark lemon yellow)

I 702 (Kelly green)

■ 310 (black)
and backstitch on
bear's mouth

Λ 666 (bright Christmas red)

·· 783 (Christmas gold)

● 414 (steel grey)

C 415 (pale grey)

H 352 (mid-peach)

		911 (mid-emerald green)
	●	798 (dark Delft blue)
	/	444 (dark lemon yellow)
	V	666 (bright Christmas red)
	C	971 (pumpkin orange)

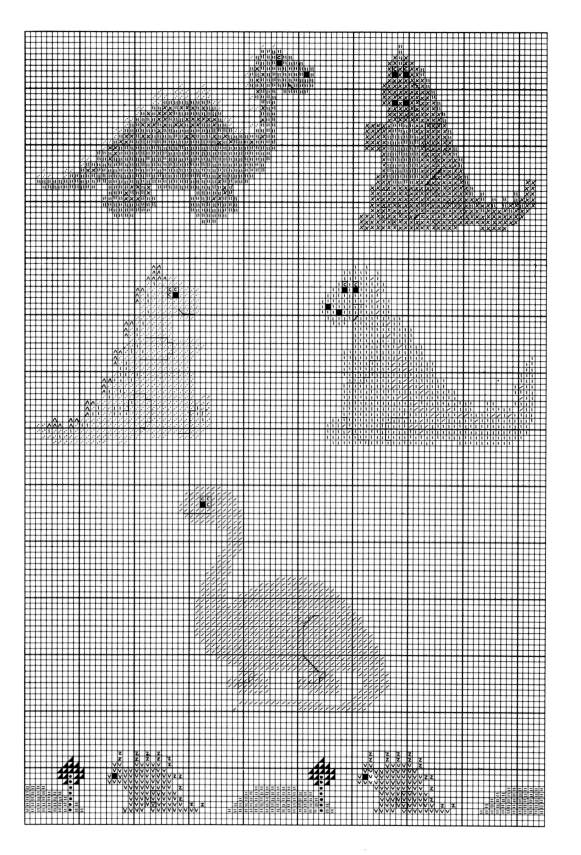

310 (black)

913 (mid-Nile green)

988 (forest green)

799 (mid-Delft blue)

610 (very dark drab brown)

899 (mid-pink)

3340 (melon orange)

white

350 (light red)

973 (bright canary yellow)

912 (light emerald green)

208 (very dark lavender)

322 (dark baby blue)

STRANDED COTTON SHADE NAMES
AND CONVERSION CHART

THE FOLLOWING CHART SHOULD BE USED AS A GUIDE ONLY BECAUSE IT IS NOT ALWAYS
POSSIBLE TO FIND EXACTLY EQUIVALENT SHADES.

SHADE NAME	DMC	ANCHOR	COATS	MADEIRA
WHITE	WHITE	1	1	WHITE
VERY DARK LAVENDER	208	111	110	0804
MID-LAVENDER	210	108	108	0802
LIGHT ROSE PINK	224	893	894	0813
VERY DARK MAHOGANY BROWN	300	352	351	2304
MID-CHRISTMAS RED	304	1006	1006	0509
BLACK	310	403	403	BLACK
MID-NAVY BLUE	311	148	149	1006
MID-STEEL GREY	317	400	400	1714
LIGHT STEEL GREY	318	399	399	1802
DARK GREEN	319	218	----	1313
MID-PISTACHIO GREEN	320	215	215	1311
CHRISTMAS RED	321	9046	9046	0510
DARK BABY BLUE	322	978	978	1004
VERY DEEP ROSE RED	326	59	----	0508
MID-ANTIQUE LILAC	327	100	100	0805
MID-BABY BLUE	334	977	977	1003
DARK PINK	335	38	38	0506
PERIWINKLE BLUE	340	118	118	0902
RED	349	13	----	0212
LIGHT RED	350	11	----	0213
DARK PEACH	351	10	----	0214
MID-PEACH	352	9	9	0303
PEACH	353	6	6	0304
LIGHT PISTACHIO GREEN	368	214	214	1310
MID-COCOA BROWN	407	914	914	2310
STEEL GREY	414	235	235	1801
PALE GREY	415	398	398	1803
MID-BROWN	433	371	----	2008
LIGHT BROWN	434	310	310	2009
VERY LIGHT BROWN	435	1046	369	2010
TAN BROWN	436	1045	368	2011
LIGHT TAN BROWN	437	362	362	2012
DARK LEMON YELLOW	444	290	291	0106
MID-AVOCADO GREEN	470	267	266	1502
LIGHT AVOCADO GREEN	471	266	265	1501
MID-OLIVE GREEN	523	859	858	1512
VERY DARK VIOLET	550	101	102	0714
DARK VIOLET	552	99	101	0713
MID-VIOLET	553	98	92	0712

Shade Name	DMC	Anchor	Coats	Madeira
Cranberry	603	62	62	0701
Light cranberry	604	55	52	0614
Bright orange red	606	335	334	0209
Bright orange	608	332	332	0206
Very dark drab brown	610	889	----	2106
Dark drab brown	611	898	----	2107
Very dark beige grey	640	903	903	1905
Dark beige grey	642	392	392	1906
Mid-beige grey	644	830	391	1907
Bright Christmas red	666	46	46	0210
Light old gold	676	891	----	2208
Very light old gold	677	886	886	2207
Dark old gold	680	901	901	2210
Bright Christmas green	700	228	229	1304
Kelly green	702	226	226	1306
Dark orange	720	326	----	0309
Pale orange	722	323	323	0307
Topaz yellow	725	305	----	0108
Light topaz yellow	726	295	295	0109
Very light topaz yellow	727	293	293	0110
Mid-old gold	729	890	890	2209
Very light tan	738	361	361	2013
Light tangerine orange	742	303	302	0114
Dark yellow	743	302	----	0113
Mid-yellow	744	301	301	0112
Very light sky blue	747	158	928	1104
Light peach	754	1012	1012	0305
Pale brick red	758	9575	336	0403
Very dark topaz brown	780	310	----	2214
Dark topaz brown	781	309	309	2213
Christmas gold	783	307	306	2211
Deep royal blue	791	178	178	0904
Blue	793	176	121	0906
Royal blue	797	132	132	0912
Dark Delft blue	798	131	131	0911
Mid-Delft blue	799	136	136	0910
Pale Delft blue	800	144	1032	0908
Dark coffee brown	801	359	358	2007
Delft blue	809	130	120	0909
Dark garnet red	814	45	43	0514
Mid-garnet red	815	43	20	0513
Garnet red	816	1005	1005	0512
Rich red	817	13	13	0211
Dark navy blue	823	152	----	1008
Dark blue	825	162	----	1011
Mid-blue	826	161	161	1012
Very dark beige brown	838	380	----	1914

Shade Name	DMC	Anchor	Coats	Madeira
Hazelnut brown	869	944	277	2105
Very dark evergreen	890	683	----	1314
Very dark coffee brown	898	360	360	2006
Mid-pink	899	52	75	0505
Mid-emerald green	911	205	----	1214
Light emerald green	912	209	205	1213
Mid-Nile green	913	204	204	1212
Dark antique blue	930	1035	922	1712
Light antique blue	932	1033	343	1710
Dark avocado green	937	268	268	1504
Dark forest brown	938	381	380	2005
Light apricot	945	881	881	2313
Burnt orange	947	330	330	0205
Very light peach	948	1011	933	0306
Aqua	959	186	186	1113
Light pumpkin orange	970	316	----	0204
Pumpkin orange	971	316	----	0203
Deep canary yellow	972	298	298	0107
Bright canary yellow	973	297	297	0105
Dark golden brown	975	355	355	2303
Mid-gold brown	976	1001	1001	2302
Forest green	988	243	----	1402
Light brown grey	3023	899	----	1902
Very light brown grey	3024	397	397	1901
Very dark brown	3031	360	----	2003
Pale golden wheat	3047	852	386	2205
Baby blue	3325	129	144	1002
Melon orange	3340	328	329	0301
Mid-yellow-green	3347	266	----	1408
Light yellow-green	3348	264	254	1409
Light loden green	3364	260	----	1603
Very dark forest brown	3371	382	----	2004
Dark mauve	3685	1028	69	0602
Mid-mauve	3688	66	60	0605